superstars!
superstars!
superstars!
superstars!

CREATIVE EDUCATION SPORTS SUPERSTARS

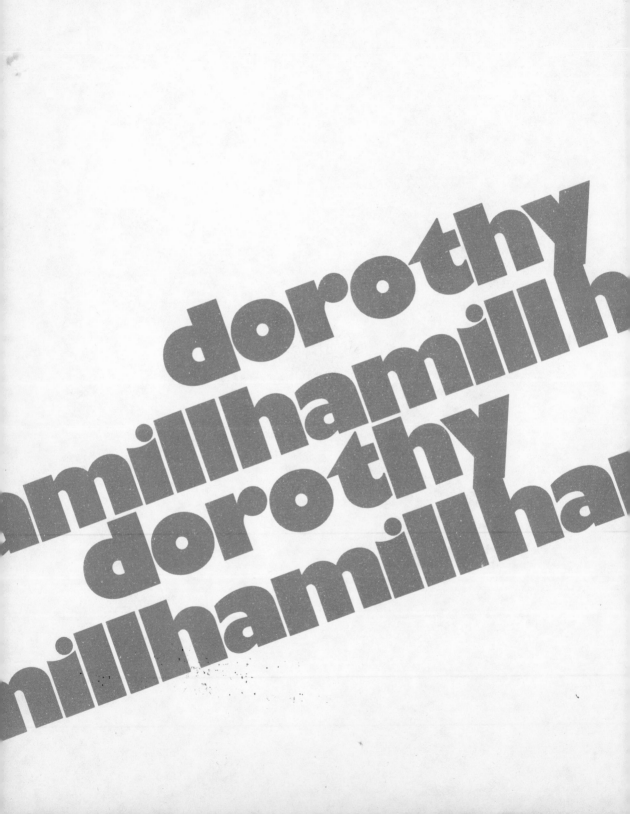

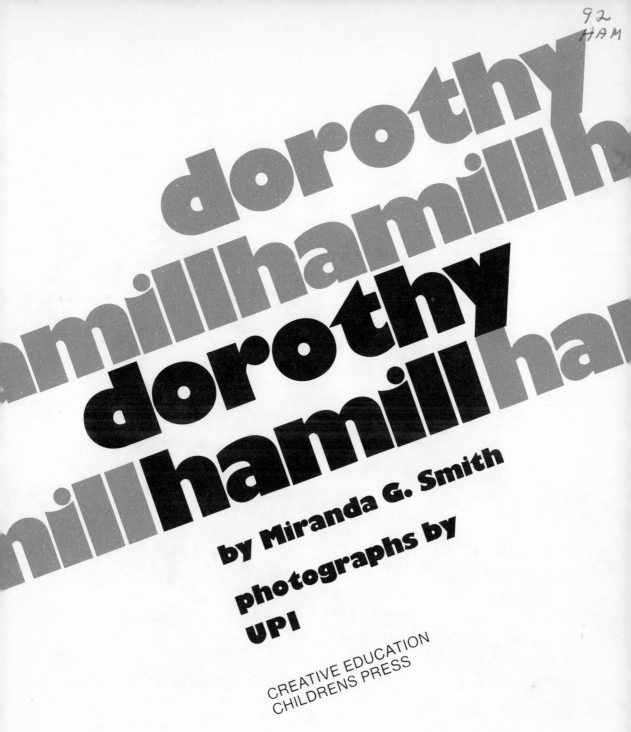

dorothy hamill

dorothy hamill

by Miranda G. Smith

photographs by

UPI

CREATIVE EDUCATION
CHILDRENS PRESS

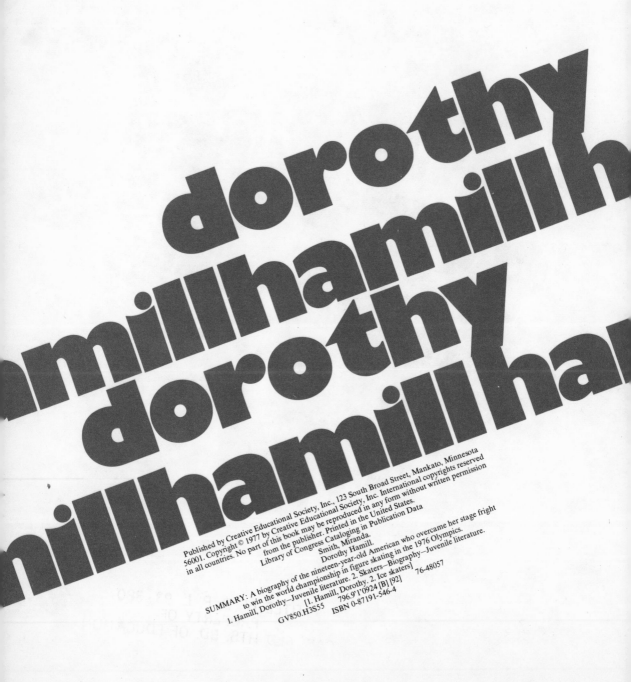

dorothy
millhamillh
amillhamillh
dorothy
millham

Published by Creative Educational Society, Inc., 123 South Broad Street, Mankato, Minnesota 56001. Copyright © 1977 by Creative Educational Society, Inc. International copyrights reserved in all countries. No part of this book may be reproduced in any form without written permission from the publisher. Printed in the United States.

Library of Congress Cataloging in Publication Data

Smith, Miranda.
Dorothy Hamill.

SUMMARY: A biography of the nineteen-year-old American who overcame her stage fright to win the world championship in figure skating in the 1976 Olympics.

1. Hamill, Dorothy—Juvenile literature. 2. Skaters—Biography—Juvenile literature.
[1. Hamill, Dorothy. 2. Ice skaters]
GV850.H3S55   796.9'1'0924 [B] [92]   76-48057
ISBN 0-87191-546-4

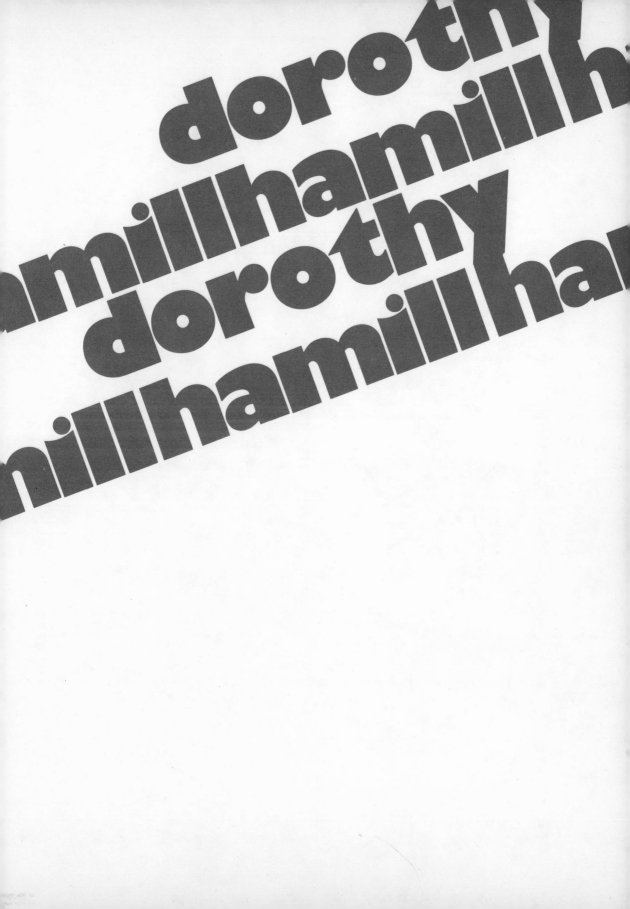

The ancient city of Innsbruck lies in a valley of Tyrol, the lovely Alpine province of Austria. The 4,500-foot high Brenner Pass, one of Europe's major travel routes, runs through the steep, snow-capped mountains which surround the city. The mountain slopes are covered with many-colored flowers in springtime, fields and meadows in summer and avid skiers in winter.

The Alps have watched over Innsbruck for centuries. The heart of the city is a maze of narrow, winding streets lined with beautiful old houses and churches whose fronts are painted in gold. Thousands of tourists visit every year to hike through or ski down the craggy mountains, stroll along the broad river Inn and explore every facet of the jewel-like city.

In February, 1976, Innsbruck was host to more visitors than ever. Thousands of people had come to watch or to take part in the Winter Olympics being held there. Cross-country skiers and ski racers, bobsledders and ski jumpers, figure skaters and speed skaters, TV crews and reporters from all over the world filled Innsbruck to overflowing.

One of the visitors was 19-year-old Dorothy Hamill, who had come all the way from her home in Riverside, Connecticut.

As soon as she arrived in Innsbruck, Dorothy felt the excitement and enchantment of the city. She longed to take the trolley through the evergreen forests around Innsbruck, and maybe ride a cablecar up to a mountaintop 6,000 feet above the city. There was so much to see and do.

But for Dorothy, sightseeing would have to wait. She was out to win the gold medal in figure skating for the United States, and she had to spend her time practicing. Dorothy worked hard on all three parts of the competition: the compulsory figures, the ''short program'' and the free-skating event. She wanted to be as perfect as possible in each of them.

There was a lot of pressure on Dorothy. She was the only American favored to win at the Winter Olympics. Bearing the hopes and expectations of a nation and being watched by the whole world would be a heavy burden for anyone. It was especially hard for Dorothy, who had always been extremely nervous in competition.

She had just won the U.S. Figure Skating Champiionships for the third straight year. But even that had not helped her confidence. The more Dorothy thought about her chances for an Olympic victory, the more doubtful she became.

First of all, she would be facing very tough competition from her two greatest rivals: Christine Errath of East Germany and Dianne de Leeuw, who was representing Holland. Errath and de Leeuw were both very strong, consistent skaters, and less bothered by tension than Dorothy. And each of them had once beaten Dorothy in the World Figure Skating Championships.

But Dorothy's biggest fear was that she might fall and ruin everything. All skaters fall sometimes. And when they do, it upsets them. But most of them don't worry much about a fall until it actually happens. Dorothy, however, has always been plagued by the possibility.

''Think how much time I've put into this, and how much other people have to help me,'' she said before the Olympics. ''With one mistake, it could all go down the drain.''

Dorothy's parents had come along to Innsbruck to give her support. It was not a new experience for them. They had been with her at every major championship she had entered. Dorothy's father was always just off the ice, ready to fix her skates or hold her hand when she needed comfort.

And her coach Carlo Fassi was also there, giving the advice and praise Dorothy needed to steady her nerves. But when the time came for her to perform in front of the judges, she would be on her own. Then she would somehow shake off her fright and concentrate only on her skating.

While the Alpine slopes were buzzing with skiing and bobsledding events, the Olympic arena in the valley below was the scene of the figure skating competitions. It was time for the first, and perhaps the most difficult and demanding, test Dorothy would face: the compulsory figures.

Doing compulsory figures means tracing perfectly proportioned circles of different, specified kinds on the ice. They have to be done first forward, then backward three times on one foot, on the inside and the outside edge of the skate blade. Then the drill is repeated on the other foot. When completed, there should be just one thin groove left forming a perfect shape.

Compulsory figures have been a part of figure skating since the sport began. Originally, skaters traced complex pictures, or even wrote their names with their

blades on the ice. Now, judges use the figures to determine the technical skill and control of each skater.

It takes many years of intensive practice to do the figures well. Even the most talented and brilliant free-skater will get nowhere if she is weak in compulsory figures.

"It can be maddening," Dorothy once said of the dull discipline, "but when you do it right, there is a certain ordered, satisfying symmetry."

Dorothy was a better free-skater than any of her competitors. But she had always had trouble in previous competitions because of the compulsory figures. When she began to train with Carlo Fassi, she became much better at them. When he decided she should use skates with flatter blades, Dorothy's figures became very good.

And that day in Innsbruck, they were excellent. Dorothy finished second to Isabel de Navarre of West Germany. Isabel always excelled in the compulsory figures, but never scored very high in the free-skating events.

Dorothy did far better in the figures than anyone had expected. And surprisingly, she was already ahead of both de Leeuw and Errath. If Dorothy continued to skate her best, it looked as if she couldn't lose.

It was expected that she would earn the highest score in the next program, a two-minute display of free-skating and compulsory jumps.

"Now you can take it easy," Dorothy's father told her. But Fassi didn't want Dorothy to play it safe. "The best defense is to attack," he replied hotly. "You can't hold anything back."

Dorothy followed her coach's advice. Her short program was fast and fiery and breathtakingly good. She leaped and flew above the ice in perfect form. The audience cheered with delight. And the judges agreed with them. They gave Dorothy very high scores, among them a rare and perfect 6.0.

Now Dorothy was far ahead of the other skaters. She could hardly believe the scores she had earned.

"It's strange — it's strange," she said in amazement. "It might really happen. I might win."

Now the last phase of the competition was just 36 hours away. The final four-minute free-skating program, a test of virtuosity and artistic ability, would determine the Olympic champion. Dorothy was in the best position to win, but steady Dianne de Leeuw was in second place and could not be counted out. Strength and determination would play a big part in the contest now. Dorothy could not afford to falter.

A reporter asked Dorothy if she would be frightened when the final program began. "No, I won't be scared, but I will be nervous," she answered. "The rest will be nervous, too. If I don't foul up, I shall do it."

Carlo Fassi wanted to make sure that Dorothy did not foul up. He knew Dorothy's biggest problem was the stage fright which gripped her before every performance.

"It's like going to an execution — your own," Dorothy once said. "I stand there in the dressing room thinking, 'Am I going to fall? Why am I doing this? I'll never do it again.' "

Although Dorothy realized her problem, she had never been able to do anything about it. Fassi decided that the best thing to do now was to seclude Dorothy from the rest of the skating team — and from her parents.

The reason for this was that Dorothy's mother was even more nervous and tense than Dorothy. She could not even watch her daughter in competition because of her anxiety. She had always stayed in their hotel room while Dorothy performed. Fassi now feared that Mrs. Hamill's jitters would be passed on to Dorothy and ruin her concentration.

So Dorothy stayed quietly in the Olympic Village and tried her best to relax. She tried not to think too much about her next trial. She kept practicing and polishing her routine.

On the night of the final program, the skating arena was packed with an excited crowd. It was the last, and the most thrilling event of the 1976 Winter Games. It was also the most expensive; some people paid more than $50 for a seat. And millions of others all over the world, who could not be in Innsbruck, huddled around their TV sets to witness the crowning of the queen of figure skating.

Many spectators at home and in the arena were cheering for their favorite, Dorothy Hamill. Ever since her appearance in the 1974 world championship, skating fans had been charmed by her.

Sometimes they had seen her quake and cry before a performance. And then they had seen her brilliant smile as she leaped and spun over the ice so beautifully. Dorothy was a very human heroine to her fans. They ached for her when she cried, and they

were overjoyed when she smiled and laughed.

They desperately wanted her to take the gold medal that night. But they were worried. In her final warm-up, Dorothy had had a bad fall. Everyone wondered if the fall could be a prediction of a bad night for her.

The anxious crowd watched intently as the first thirteen skaters presented their programs. There were many very talented performers on the ice that evening. And they all won warm applause.

But then came the moment the audience had so eagerly awaited. It was Dorothy's turn now. Backstage, she was trembling with fright. But as her name was announced, Dorothy stood straight with determination and pushed off onto the ice.

When she saw the crowd cheering and holding up signs for her, Dorothy broke into tears. Letting out the bottled-up tension seemed to help her calm down at last. A bright smile lit her face as the music for her routine began.

Dorothy moved about the rink with graceful, flowing rhythm. Her jumps were high and smooth and looked effortless. A feeling of enchantment filled the arena. As the seconds ticked by, there was a surge of relief throughout the crowd. It was clear that Dorothy was at her best and would not fall.

Her program consisted of many intricate moves which have strange-sounding names. There were walley jumps and double-axels, double-toe loops and delayed axels, double-salchows and double-lutzes. She also did splits and a Bauer spiral, a delayed double-salchow, a camelspin and a lay-back spin. Dorothy's program ended with her "signature", a "Hamill camel" — a camelspin into a sitspin.

The audience cheered long and loud and tossed bouquets of spring flowers all over the rink. Dorothy skated around proudly, picking up the flowers and beaming at her fans. Three girls came out to help her collect the mass of color and clear the rink for the next skater.

Dorothy's scores were proof of her fine performance. She was awarded eight 5.8's and a 5.9 (out of a possible 6.0) for technical merit, and all 5.9's for artistic interpretation. Dorothy wasn't wearing her glasses, and she could hardly see the scoreboard. But the joyous reaction of the audience told her that she was in the lead.

Back in the dressing room, Dorothy was hugged by her father, her coach and friends. She was surprised by her own performance. "I didn't really bomb out on anything," she said. "That's a first for me!"

Dianne de Leeuw had not yet performed, but she

knew that even the greatest performance of her life would not bring her any more than second place that night. Dorothy was just that far ahead.

Dorothy was radiant as she stood on the winner's platform. "The Star-Spangled Banner" played as the mayor of Innsbruck placed the gold medal around Dorothy's neck. It was the joyous fulfillment of all her years of hard work and tears.

"This is worth all the terrible moments of worry in the dressing room," she exclaimed. "I wouldn't give it up for anything."

Dorothy wore her gold medal to dinner. When she finally got to bed early the next morning, it was close by under her pillow. And the next day, when someone asked her where it was, Dorothy pulled the medal on its striped ribbon out of her blouse. "Right here," she laughed.

At last it was time for Dorothy to take a rest. Now she could spend some time touring the golden city of Innsbruck and the lofty mountains which guard it.

Dorothy's vacation was not to last for long. Soon she was training again, this time for the 1976 World Figure Skating Championships to be held in Güteborg, Sweden. She was determined to win the title which had eluded her for two years.

When Dorothy first went to the world championships in 1974, she had just won her first U.S. National Figure-skating title. She was new to international competition and to skating fans. But she would soon become well known and loved.

The 1974 world championship was nearing its end; it was the night of the final free-skating performances. Dorothy was nervously waiting at the edge of the rink for her name to be announced and her music to begin.

Suddenly the audience began to boo the low scores the previous skater had just been given. Dorothy burst into tears and ran off the ice to her father. She thought the crowd was booing her.

When she realized she was wrong, Dorothy wiped away her tears and went bravely back onto the ice. When the music started, she was smiling. And her skating was as brilliant as her smile.

Christine Errath won the world title that night, but Dorothy had won the hearts of countless fans.

Dorothy returned in 1975. She put on a fine performance and excelled in every event. But when she fell during a sitspin, the world title went to Dianne de Leeuw. Again Dorothy finished second.

In March of 1976, however, the odds were in Dorothy's favor. Winning the Olympic gold medal had given her new confidence and determination.

She scored second to Isabel de Navarre in the compulsory figures. And in both the short program and the free-skating event, Dorothy was judged the best. Her total score made her the first American world champion since Peggy Fleming, who won the title in 1968. Now there was no doubt that Dorothy Hamill was the best figure skater in the world.

The American public was very proud of her. And when she returned to the U.S., Dorothy was greeted enthusiastically wherever she went.

In New York, she was honored by the National Women's Republican Club. First Lady Betty Ford presented Dorothy with the club's Outstanding Young Woman of the Year award.

There was even more in store for Dorothy when she came home to Greenwich, Connecticut. Dorothy had grown up in the suburb of Riverside, but it seemed as if the residents of the whole city, and many other towns as well, had turned out to greet her that day.

Thousands of people were crowding the streets, overflowing the squares and parks, perching on rooftops and dangling from trees. They were all waiting to get a glimpse of Dorothy as she rode triumphantly through the streets in a motorcade.

Dorothy was bubbling with excitement and pleasure. Wherever she rode, a deafening chorus of cheers filled her ears. And whenever the car stopped, she was surrounded by admirers shouting her name and trying to touch her.

Dorothy signed as many autographs as she could. After a while her hand was aching, but she didn't mind. Many years before, she had tried to get a skating star's autograph, but failed. Dorothy now tried to sign every autograph she was asked for. She knew the bitter disappointment of being refused.

The motorcade stopped at the pond where Dorothy first began to skate. There a plaque was dedicated to her. Then everyone proceeded to the Greenwich skating rink. It was formally renamed in Dorothy's honor. And when she said, "If it encourages people to skate for fun, that's all I can hope for," she was cheered again. All day long the town held ceremonies

to pay tribute to Dorothy Hamill.

Dorothy's appeal was not limited to the East Coast. Girls all over the country rushed to get their hair cut short like hers. They sent her loads of fan mail. And everywhere there was a new surge of interest in skating.

Dorothy was overwhelmed and thrilled by her popularity. She had scarcely dreamed that things would turn out this way when her skating career began.

Dorothy got her first pair of skates for Christmas when she was eight years old. She went to the nearby pond to try them out. After a while she saw someone skating backwards, and she wanted to learn to do that, too. And when she saw somebody else doing a spin, Dorothy was hooked. She begged her parents for lessons. They told her, ''If you want to skate, that's fine — as long as you work hard.''

And Dorothy did work hard. Soon she was getting up before dawn to practice seven hours a day, six days a week. At 14, she got permission to leave school so that she could train and compete more freely. In her hours off the ice, Dorothy studied with a private tutor and completed her education. She seldom saw her older brother and sister because of her travels to train with the best coaches available.

"I don't even know what it's like to be normal," Dorothy once said, "but I've never really found anything I liked to do as much as skating."

Dorothy's skating improved a lot when she went to Denver, Colorado to train with Carlo Fassi. She joined over 30 other American and foreign skaters who were studying with him.

Fassi, now considered the best figure skating coach in the world, has been a great help to many skaters. He coached Peggy Fleming, the 1968 Olympic gold medal winner. Another of his students is John Curry of Great Britain, who won the men's Olympic title in 1976.

Fassi is an energetic yet calm man. He is especially good at reassuring his skaters when they are feeling defeated and blue.

"To make a champion, I have to be patient," he says. "With Dorothy, it is not always easy. She gets mad at herself."

Fassi had to combat Dorothy's lack of self-confidence. He knew that even the most gifted athlete cannot survive the tough world of competition on skill alone; what separates the champions from the rest is the enormous amount of confidence they have in themselves.

But Dorothy was one of the very rare exceptions to the rule. She was never content with her skating. "I think I look lousy," she would say.

She tried Fassi's patience. "She is critical of herself to the point of being negative," he once said. "I keep telling her that if you want to convince the judges that you're the best, you must first convince yourself."

Fassi helped Dorothy relax a bit and smooth out her skating style. He also improved her compulsory figures tremendously.

"Before I got to Carlo, I was tied up in knots doing figures," Dorothy once told an interviewer. "I looked like a pretzel."

And after her Olympic victory, Dorothy said, "I owe 75 percent of my gold medal to Carlo."

All Dorothy's hard work has made her a great skater.

Figure skating judge Charles Foster has this to say about her style: "Dorothy skates with finesse; she performs a difficult program, works at high speed, plus she interprets the music with feeling. She's a beautiful skater."

Former Olympic champion Dick Button agrees. "Every move is right, every line is clean," he said. "Everything is in the right position."

But Dorothy is more than skillful. She has a deep feeling for her sport. And her distinctive skating is truly a work of art.

What makes Dorothy such an exciting skater is the spontaneity of all her moves. Most skaters make certain obvious movements which tell the audience when they are about to jump. But Dorothy's moves are very subtle and smooth. She just seems to take flight and hang suspended in mid-air before coming gently back down to the ice.

She is famous for her spins. They are at high speed yet look very delicate and effortless, as though some force other than her own were twirling her. And every move she makes flows with the music as if the melody were coming from inside her.

One reason Dorothy is so good is her ability to totally control her body. Dorothy loves ballet; and like a fine dancer, she has trained herself to perform smoothly and precisely.

She loves her work. "You're skating and doing the most difficult things," she has said, "and the audience is with you. They're clapping, cheering. You're floating. It's like nothing else I've ever felt."

After winning the world championship, Dorothy announced that her competitive career was over. But she will still be very much in the spotlight.

She has signed a contract to do television commercials and two TV specials in 1976. She has also joined the Ice Capades and will be earning a very high salary.

Dorothy has already won more fame and success than most people achieve in a lifetime. And no matter what she accomplishes from now on, her remarkable golden victory at Innsbruck will be praised for many years to come.

But after all is said and done, the fame and tribute she has received remain of secondary importance to Dorothy.

"I skate for myself and not anybody else," she says. "On the ice I'm in a different world, and everything is smooth and breezy and shiny."

Football
Johnny Unitas
Bob Griese
Vince Lombardi
Joe Namath
O. J. Simpson
Fran Tarkenton
Roger Staubach
Alan Page
Larry Csonka
Don Shula
Franco Harris
Terry Bradshaw
Chuck Foreman

Baseball
Frank Robinson
Tom Seaver
Jackie Robinson
Johnny Bench
Hank Aaron
Roberto Clemente
Mickey Mantle
Rod Carew
Fred Lynn
Pete Rose

Basketball
Walt Frazier
Kareem Abdul Jabbar
Wilt Chamberlain
Jerry West
Bill Russell
Bill Walton
Bob McAdoo
Julius Erving
John Havlicek
Rick Barry
George McGinnis

superstars!
superstars
superstars
superstars

CREATIVE EDUCATION SPORTS SUPERSTARS

Golf
Lee Trevino
Jack Nicklaus
Arnold Palmer
Johnny Miller
Kathy Whitworth
Laura Baugh

Miscellaneous
Mark Spitz
Muhammad Ali
Secretariat
Olga Korbut
Evel Knievel
Jean Claude Killy
Janet Lynn
Peggy Fleming
Pelé
Rosi Mittermaier
Sheila Young
Dorothy Hamill
Nadia Comaneci

Hockey
Phil and Tony Esposito
Gordie Howe
Bobby Hull
Bobby Orr

Tennis
Jimmy Connors
Chris Evert
Pancho Gonzales
Evonne Goolagong
Arthur Ashe
Billie Jean King
Stan Smith

Racing
Peter Revson
Jackie Stewart
A. J. Foyt
Richard Petty